MW01616076

what is Modesty?

discovering the truth

Michelle Brock

Managing Editor, Beneth Perry
Cover & Content Layout, Allison Pust
Illustrations, Sarah Forsythe
Iron Sharpeneth Iron Publications
Newberry Springs, California

A Note From the Author

Thanks to all those who gave ideas, comments, and criticism. Your feedback was immensely helpful. Thank you especially to my husband, brother, and father, who had the courage to be brutal! The changes you recommended were well appreciated. Thanks also to Pastor Needham and the young ladies using this material as a Bible study, and Mark and Charity, whose encouraging comments sparked much discussion at our household and sent me back to work to communicate more clearly. This book grew out of a presentation my mom first gave when I was in high school. More than anything else, this book is a reflection of years of time and energy my mom has invested in my life. Beginning long before I can remember, she has modeled these principles, discussed them with me, and helped me apply them.

About the Author

Michelle graduated with a B.A. in English and an M.Ed. in Special Education from Bob Jones University. This presentation was originally given to college girls while Michelle was teaching at Maranatha Baptist Bible College. She now enjoys her full-time job as the wife of Lee and the mother of David and Bethel.

Table of Contents

1

Modesty
Defined

Which article of clothing above do you think is the *most* God-honoring?

Which one is the *least* God-honoring?

Here's another question: when you think of modest clothing, what other words come to your mind?

Ugly   *Plain*   *Out of style*

Sloppy   *Sexy*   *Beautiful*   *Stylish*

Can you describe a modest person? Maybe you think of a mousy, quiet soul with no personality, or an unattractive woman who is proud of how she dresses and is openly critical of anyone who differs from her style in the least bit. Do you think of a beautiful woman at all? How about the way she acts? Does that factor into your assessment of her modesty?

Your answers to these questions reveal to some degree how you understand the concept of modesty.

Because many people (including Christians) have difficulty understanding what modesty is, we should begin by establishing a good definition of modesty. It is helpful to begin by examining how a modern dictionary describes modesty. The American Heritage Dictionary says that modesty is "reserve or propriety in speech, dress, or behavior."

Because most of us think of clothing when we consider the word *modesty*, it is important to notice that this definition includes more than simply what a person wears. It involves speech and behavior as well as dress. This definition is actually consistent with what we find in the Bible.

In fact, you might be surprised to see how the Bible defines modesty. Let's take a closer look at the Bible to see how God describes this modest person we Christians are supposed to be.

The first key to understanding a biblical definition is that modesty is not merely what you wear. Modesty is not a "good" article of clothing, and immodesty is not a "bad" article of clothing. Actually, modesty is quite different. Biblical modesty is more about what you *are* than what you wear.

We draw our current understanding of modesty from several biblical concepts, including the biblical word *modest* (KJV), which refers to appropriateness. In passages that deal with how Christian women should dress and act, we see humility and purity emphasized as well as appropriateness. It is significant that none of these words refer to specific articles of clothing. Let us look briefly at some verses that use these words, come to a conclusion on a definition, and then discuss the parts of the definition in more detail.

 *Humility*

I Peter 3:2-6—Whose adorning let it not be that outward adorning of plaiting the hair, and of wearing of gold, or of putting on of apparel; but let it be the hidden man of the heart, in that which is not corruptible, even the ornament of a meek and quiet spirit, which is in the sight of God of great price. For after this manner in the old time the holy women also, who trusted in God, adorned themselves, being in subjection unto their own husbands: even as Sara obeyed Abraham, calling him lord: whose daughters ye are, as long as ye do well, and are not afraid with any amazement.

Peter instructs Christian ladies to adorn themselves with a meek and quiet spirit. A meek spirit in this context is a spirit of humility. Peter illustrates this attitude by describing godly women who in humility placed themselves under the authority of their husbands. The grace of humility is essential for submitting to authority and is a rare and precious adornment for a Christian lady. It affects why we do what we do, including why we choose certain clothes and how we wear them. No matter how we dress, if we are filled with pride in our "modesty" and superior disdain for others who dress differently (even if we believe they are wrong), we show that we misunderstand what modesty really is.

In several modern Jewish books on modesty, the authors describe humility as a crucial element in deciding what they wear. They point out that the modern Hebrew word for modesty is the corresponding word that is translated *humble* in the Old Testament passage of *Micah 6:8*: "What does the Lord require of thee? But to do justly and to love mercy and to walk *humbly* [modestly] with thy God." This idea is consistent with passages in 1Peter and 1Timothy that indicate that modesty is not compatible with showy, excessive attention to appearance. In other words, pride is not modest, but humility is.

Titus 2:4-5—That they may teach the young women to be sober, to love their husbands, to love their children, to be discreet, chaste, keepers at home, good, obedient to their own husbands, that the word of God be not blasphemed.

1 Peter 3:2-4— While they behold your chaste conversation coupled with fear. Whose adorning let it not be that outward adorning of plaiting the hair, and of

wearing of gold, or of putting on of apparel; But let it
be the hidden man of the heart, in that which is not
corruptible, even the ornament of a meek and quiet
spirit, which is in the sight of God of great price.

In the Bible, *pure* is often translated *chaste* (KJV). Notice that purity is something that comes out in our lifestyle—the word *conversation* in 1 Peter means behavior or our lifestyle. We have a tendency to limit purity to sexual purity, especially when it concerns what we wear, primarily because purity can be expressed through what we wear. We talk a lot about purity, such as saving your body for your husband or not doing anything sexually that we would regret or that is outside God's clear rules for sexuality. But purity encompasses far more than just sexual purity.

Hebrews 12:1 tells us to get rid of anything that hinders our walk with God. James talks about staying unspotted from the world *(James 1:27).* A person who finds his speech is beginning to be characterized by sarcasm and innuendo may determine that he needs to limit the television he watches. And a young lady may be surprised to realize that the unsaved coworkers she spends time with after work are affecting her desire to serve the Lord with her family. These examples illustrate the importance of this concept of chaste, or pure, living. Have you ever done something wrong that leaves a yucky feeling in your stomach every time you think of it? Would you want a sinful choice you made to limit the effectiveness you could have for the Lord? So although chaste living does include purity, it implies much more, including our lifestyle, thought processes, and desires.

Appropriateness

1 Timothy 2:9—In like manner also, that women adorn themselves in modest apparel, with shamefacedness and sobriety; not with braided hair, or gold, or pearls, or costly array; but (which becometh women professing godliness) with good works.

Finally, we must make appropriate choices in our clothing and behavior. Having a heart that is humble and pure is the first step to modesty. Now we must apply these principles to specific situations.

1Timothy 2:9 is the only verse that contains the English word *modest* in the Bible. So, whatever modesty means here, we Christian ladies are supposed to dress this way. The apostle Paul is not talking about a particular style; the Greek word for *modest* in this context actually means *appropriate.* Paul clarifies his meaning by contrasting the word translated *modest* (and its synonyms *shamefacedness* and *sobriety*) with examples of immodesty. The elaborate, over-the-top hair, jewelry, and clothes were excessive, too much—in stark contrast to the concept of modesty that Paul was trying to teach. Compare this verse with *1 Peter 3:2-4*, which also contrasts excessive attention to appearance with a godly lifestyle. Both Paul and Peter wanted Christian ladies to dress appropriately, with restraint.

Proverbs 11:22 says, "As a jewel of gold in a swine's snout, so is a fair woman which is without discretion." Knowing what is appropriate isn't always easy. That is why discretion is so important. A beautiful woman without the ability to make good judgments about what to do, say, and wear is just as mixed up as putting valuable earrings on a smelly pig. Knowing what to do in a situation takes good taste—seeing all the facts, deciding what facts are important, and even knowing what is beautiful and attractive. In the church today, God wants us to grow through the exercise of discernment based on biblical principles. Paul describes this skill when he says, "Prove all things; hold fast that which is good" *(1 Thessalonians 5:21).*

If we take all of these words—humility, purity, and appropriateness—and put them together, we get a good picture of our current understanding of *modesty.* Here are some ways that we can describe modesty.

Modesty is an attitude of humility that seeks to please God rather than man or self. It is characterized by restraint and self-control, and dignity in dress, speech, and actions.

 *Modesty is a product of pure thinking and is not determined by what you wear. You don't become modest simply by putting on a "modest" dress.*

 *Being appropriate requires discretion to evaluate what is modest in each situation.*

 *Although it is not true that modesty equals clothing, it is true that what we wear and how we wear it can be modest or immodest.*

> To sum up, modesty is a way of thinking that is characterized by humility and purity, and results in appropriate actions.

We must now attempt to put into practice these principles we find from God's Word. Sometimes the application is easy, like getting rid of a t-shirt that is too tight. Other times, the application is more challenging, like changing how we think or talk about men. Following a list of rules is far easier than the difficult process of learning to apply principles. It is often a lazy substitute for the careful study and application of God's Word. We should strive to be like the Bereans who were commended for their excited diligence in searching Scripture to verify the truth that they were being shown.

Remember that God did not give us a list of complex rules, complete with a vast index, to live the Christian life. There simply isn't enough space to give step-by-step instructions for every variation of every situation a particular person will experience in her lifetime. Instead, God gave us the Bible, complete with principles that apply to every variation of every situation a person will experience.

The elements of modesty we will study can all be expressed through what we wear. Although many of the examples you will find here are clothing examples, keep in mind that while specifically identifying clothing applications can be helpful, they do not substitute for the emphasis on the heart attitudes that are discussed throughout

Scripture. It is far better for each of us to prayerfully take principles from God's Word and apply them personally and specifically to our lives than to mindlessly follow a list of rules.

2

Modesty is Humble

Some women struggle with pride in their clothing by being overly concerned about what other people will think of how they dress. They want to be admired rather than silently scorned for what they are wearing. These ladies attempt to stay at the cutting edge of fashion sometimes simply because they don't want people to think they are out of style. The primary motivation in their clothing choices is, "What will my fashion conscious friends think of me?"

Many of these Christian ladies are careful not to dress in the more sexually alluring items of clothing. Their ability to find "modest" clothing that is also in style is admirable. The clothing in this case may not be the problem at all. Rather, the problem is in the *motivation* behind buying and wearing the clothing, whether you are wearing an attractive hand-sewn jumper to please your jumper friends or wearing a new pair of $100 brand-name slacks with your 'in' friends. These are examples of immodest motives.

When other people's opinions control the choices we make, we are demonstrating what the Bible calls the fear of man. *Proverbs 25:29* says that the fear of man brings a snare, a trap. We get into all kinds of trouble when we make decisions based primarily on what others think of us. It is sin because we make other people the ruler of our lives (an idol) instead of God.

Women who are driven by what others think of them (fear of man) may occasionally choose clothing that is a little too short, a little too clingy, or a little too low-cut in their attempts to be stylish. Or they may wear sexy clothing because that's how they want to be perceived. They like the admiration they believe they receive when they dress in a certain way. Notice the motivation. It is self-directed and prideful.

Why do you think women like to dress in style? Many women like to be attractive to their friends and tend to choose clothes they know their friends will approve of or like. Sometimes, though, women are trapped by their desire for approval. They might buy something quite stylish that doesn't look good on them. The color might make them look washed out, or the style might be a poor choice for their shape of body and face. Wanting to look attractive isn't the problem.

The problem begins when a woman cares more about what her friends think than whether the outfit actually looks good, and ultimately, whether it is pleasing to the Lord.

It's not that what people think is completely irrelevant. The apostle Paul tells us not to let our good be evil spoken of *(Romans 14:16)*. The Roman Christians were selfishly defending their rights without any concern at all for how their actions were being perceived by other believers. Paul acknowledged that the activity in question may not have been sinful, but he did not excuse their disregard for the impact of their actions on other believers' spiritual lives. In order to apply this principle to our lives, we *must* be aware of what others think and how it influences the way that they think about God. The difference between the fear of man and a godly awareness of others is our motivation. Ungodly fear of man seeks to please self. A godly consideration of others seeks to please God and build up other believers *(Romans 14:19)*.

The Pharisees were keenly aware of what people thought of them. They cared more about pleasing men than pleasing God *(John 12:43)*. We often do the same thing, leading to unwise decisions or decisions that are made for sinful motives.

Women who want to be discerning often see other women making some of these errors and wisely try to avoid making them themselves. At the same time, many of these women take great pride in the fact that they themselves dress modestly. True, they are rightly committed to pleasing the Lord by how they dress and may actually wear stylish and attractive clothing. But their heart motives for doing so are seriously corrupted by their pride.

Women who choose to wear plain or shapeless clothing because they assume this is more spiritual err in much the same way. Regardless of the clothing choices either of these two types of women make, they want others to notice their modest dress and admire their commitment to spirituality. They are very likely critical of others who dress differently, believing that a woman who does not ascribe to their particular definition of modesty cannot please the Lord in any area of her life. These wrong assumptions and motivations are just as prideful as the others.

The bottom line is, if we are proud of how we dress,

we are immodest, no matter how long our skirts.

A humble woman may disagree with another's view of modesty, but she is careful how and when she communicates her opinion. And she understands that God works in different ways and times for each of us. She knows that modesty isn't always easily defined and understands that her own understanding of modesty has developed as she has matured as a woman and a child of God. She is patient and gracious to others, but she also recognizes that others who dress differently may have something spiritual to teach her.

A woman who dresses modestly because she fears God and delights to please Him wisely understands how much God hates prideful motives and pharisaical comparisons that exalt man rather than God. She doesn't abandon modest clothing to avoid being self-righteous. Rather, she abandons self-exalting motives and the critical spirit that is associated with pride and is so offensive to God.

This modest woman is just as careful in how she dresses as the other ladies we have described. Her motivation, however, is very different, even if she chooses some of the same clothes. Instead of worrying what her friends think of her, she is careful to consider first God's desires for her life. She is aware of how she is perceived, for example, by unsaved and saved alike, with a desire to be a good testimony. She chooses attractive clothing because it reflects the character of God, not because she wants to turn heads.

No matter what motivates us to buy or wear clothes, we must remember that modesty encompasses what we think and how we act as well as what we wear. Humility should be present in every area of our lives if we want to be modest. Then, when we consider the area of clothing, our hearts will be ready to make wise choices for the right reasons. When we are humble, we will be far more gracious and patient with others who are learning (or have not yet learned) some of the same things God has already taught us.

How can I be humble in my clothing?

Before you buy an article of clothing, consider your motivation. Is it more important to you to please your friends than to submit to your parents or other authority? Is the approval of your friends more important to you than the approval of God? How often does your taste in clothing differ from your friends or from what is in style? It's not that having clothes your friends like is bad; but if you have difficulty buying something you like because you know your friends won't like it, you may be struggling with the fear of man. The book *When People Are Big and God Is Small* by Ed Welch describes how the fear of man affects nearly every part of us, and explains how replacing fear of man with the fear of God can overcome this bondage.

Try going shopping with your friends but not buying clothing with them. This is drastic, but if you are trying to limit the influence of your friends, it can be helpful. Friends often tell you what you want to hear instead of what you need to hear. Friends also have a tendency to approve clothing that they like or looks good on them and not necessarily what looks good on you. Once as a teenager I asked a girl her opinion of an outfit I was going to wear, and she said it looked fine. When I later decided it wasn't acceptable and changed, she said, "Oh I thought you needed to change, too. I just didn't want you to feel bad." This kind of friend is not helpful!

Next ask how you think of those whose clothing choices differ from yours. Are you tempted to criticize or make fun of people that you think look dowdy? Does a person's view on clothing affect your entire attitude toward her? If so, it may be that you are not humbly allowing God to work in others' lives in His time.

Amazingly, God uses sinners to teach us about Him.

If we expected our sisters in Christ to be perfect (according to our standard) when God does not expect perfection of them, what does that say about our estimation of ourselves?

Clothing Worn in Humility is Beautiful

Does humility mean that you must dress in dull colors and outdated styles? Are denim jumpers the only acceptable dress for a Christian? Must you lose your individuality in a sea of plain conformity?

Applying humility to our clothing choices does not mean that ugliness is spiritual. Modesty doesn't mean God wants you to be ugly. Ugly clothing actually can be immodest. Does ugliness reflect the character of God when God obviously loves beauty?

Look at the world He created. God is not boring! Look at the detail, the color, the texture, and the variety. Artists study long years to learn principles of harmony and beauty that are reflected in the world around us. God is the master artist. He could have made a bright red sky with orange grass, but He didn't. The blue, green, and earth tones of God's creation are perfectly designed for the comfort of our eyes. Try changing your color scheme on your computer from neutral colors to red and orange. There's a reason for the gray and blue that makes up most of the color on our screens. Just like the grass and sky, which make up such a large part of our outside world, the typical colors of our computer screens are also pleasant to look at and tend to reflect the color balance of creation, especially for those who look at a computer screen for hours in a day. God's artistry in creation is evident wherever you look.

If we want to reflect who God is in our lives, our clothing will also reflect the variety of creation. Christians don't have to wear the same colors and styles any more than there is only one color for the birds. How many different colors and types of birds did God make just because they were beautiful? Does every bird have to be bright red? Or brown? Not every person must dress in bright colors any more than every person should dress in darker colors. There's room for individuality in God's world.

There are other ways we know that attractive clothing can be modest. Look at the *Proverbs 31* woman. She is often given as an example of a godly, virtuous woman. How did she dress? Verse 22 tells us "her clothing is silk and purple." Not only did this godly woman choose beautiful colors, she also chose beautiful fabrics as well.

Moreover, her clothing choices are given as an *admirable* characteristic. This is one more way we know spirituality does not demand ugly attire.

There's room for individuality in God's world

God gives us another example of beauty in His creation. When God told Moses to build the tabernacle, He gave specific instructions on materials, measurements, and decorations. God does not leave us wondering why He gave the directions He did. *Hebrews 8:5* tells us that the tabernacle was an "example and shadow of heavenly things." This verse says that everything in the tabernacle represents something about God and His relationship to His people. When you look at God's instructions for the tabernacle, you can see that He designed it as a place of beauty and holiness. If you look at many of the instructions, you find very quickly that many parts of the tabernacle sound gorgeous: with vibrant color, gold plating, and so on. God's tabernacle was set apart not just by its status as a holy place but also by its transcendent beauty. It is interesting that God calls our bodies His temple in *1 Corinthians 6:19.* Following this thought, we should adorn this temple in a way that reflects the beauty of God.

Now look at something very interesting. In *Exodus 28:2*, we are told that even the garments the priests wore in the tabernacle were to be fashioned both for glory (honor) and beauty. Why would God care about making the garment beautiful? One reason might be found in a phrase David uses several times in his Psalms. *Psalm 29:2* says, "Give unto the Lord the glory due unto his name; worship the Lord in the *beauty of holiness*."

David describes God's holiness as beautiful. You could say that beauty is a reflection of God's perfect holiness. Do you think of God's holiness as beautiful?

Looking beautiful is far more than choosing colors and styles that look good on you, although this information can be quite helpful to learn. Taking the time to be clean and well-groomed is also a part of looking attractive. Some women have a harder time than others caring about whether they look nice. And learning to care about good grooming is often a part of growing up. When you go somewhere

Can you act and dress in such a way that shows both holiness and beauty?

that you know you won't see anybody you know, are you tempted to dress sloppily or leave your hair unkempt? If our primary motivation for looking beautiful is to reflect God's character, it will not matter who sees us. God is pleased when the motivation behind our choices is simply to honor Him.

It is helpful to remember that it is sometimes appropriate (and therefore *modest* and *holy*) to get dirty. We would not say that it is ungodly to get dirt under your fingernails while you are pulling weeds in your yard. A baby might spit up on his mother's shirt, and she might simply wash it off with a cloth instead of changing right away. There are appropriate times to spend more or less time on our clothing, hair, and makeup. One way to evaluate whether your appearance is appropriate or not is to examine your motivation for your care (or lack thereof). Do you have a reason for your appearance? For example, you might put off washing your hair first thing in the morning because you plan to shower after you exercise. You might run to the store to buy some garden supplies looking grubby because you plan to go right back to working in the dirt when you get home. The motives here may be simple efficiency and stewardship of time. If your appearance results from laziness or selfishness or reflects a carelessness of how you are perceived by others, you may want to re-examine how you make yourself look presentable in these situations.

But what if you don't feel very beautiful? Does this mean that you are somehow less godly just because you don't look like a model? Not at all. You and I are a part of God's creation and exactly like God wanted us! We can say with David, "I will praise thee; for I am fearfully *and* wonderfully made: marvellous *are* thy works; and *that* my soul knoweth right well" *(Psalm 139:14)*. Yes, there are variations in physical beauty; but as we saw in chapter one, Peter and Paul make it clear that the most important part of our beauty comes from inside us. At the beginning of this chapter, we said that humility doesn't mean we have to look ugly. We're talking about motives for taking care of (or not) the outside of us. A heart that desires to please God will desire to reflect His character. Because of the Holy Spirit that lives within us, we have the ability and responsibility to choose what is pure and lovely whenever we can *(Philippians 1:9-11)*. Because physical beauty isn't anything we have a choice about, it isn't covered in this command.

However, we do make choices about our appearance every day. We choose what clothes to put on, whether to eat three candy bars for breakfast every day, whether to comb our hair, and so on. It is these choices that can be important.

Women can also be a *poor* testimony by not taking care of themselves and how they dress. When younger girls who want to do right look at how you dress, do they think, "I like modesty" or do they think, "Modesty is ugly"? When they are old enough to be making clothing choices on their own, will they be challenged by your example or be repulsed by your example? This is not the prideful fear of man we talked about earlier. Remember that we are the children of God who represent God in the world, and how other believers respond to our lives is biblically important.

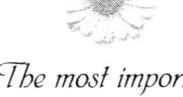

The most important part of our beauty comes from inside us.

Taking care to find clothing that is beautiful *is* important, because beauty is a part of who God is. The more like God we become, the better we will be able to evaluate true beauty.

How Can I Choose Beautiful Adornment (clothing, hair, makeup and hygiene)?

1 Consciously look for beauty in what you wear. Yes, there will be differences in taste, but it is wrong to look for ugly clothes. It is the desire to be pleasing to God that is significant here, not whether you have bad taste or not.

2 Realize that beauty in what we wear is not forbidden. It is not sinful to look for and wear beautiful clothing, because beauty is a reflection of God's character.

3 Take the time to find what colors and styles of clothing look good on you. When I was a teenager, the book *Color Me Beautiful* by Carole Jackson was popular among Christians because it gives practical ideas for choosing clothing based on what complements your hair and skin color.

Have a makeover done by someone who is knowledgeable in these matters (not just someone who wants to sell you the latest colors and styles). Take your mom with you.

 Avoid looking sloppy. The grunge look may be stylish, but it doesn't seem to fit commands in the Bible to be orderly. *1Corinthians 14:40* says, "Let all things be done decently and in order." How should this verse affect what you wear?

 Take the time to be well-groomed. You may not spend an hour fixing your hair every day, but making sure it is clean and combed is important.

 Recognize that your testimony is important. As Christians, we represent our Lord. Is our appearance contradicting the One we represent?

 Dress appropriately for the tasks at hand. How you dress when you are at home and not likely to see anyone else may not be a spiritual issue. However, you may find that you are more productive if you take the time to get ready for your day, instead of staying in your pajamas all day long.

3

Modesty is
Always Pure and
Sometimes Sexy

If we are to reflect God's holiness in how we dress, how can modesty be sexy and pure at the same time? First we must understand what God's holiness is all about, because our understanding of purity is based on God's holiness. When the Bible says that God is holy, it means that God is set apart from anything bad. We are to be separate from sin, or holy, in the same way. *1 Peter 1:15* tells us that we are to be holy in "all manner of conversation," or in every area of our lives.

What is being *sexy? Being sexy is doing, saying, or wearing anything that draws attention to my sexuality.* Another word for being sexy is *sensual.* Sexy or sensual clothing is clothing that draws attention to a woman's sexual body parts, like her breasts, rear, legs, and so on.

Now, many women incorrectly believe that being sexy, or desiring to be sexy, is sinful and definitely unholy. What they do not realize or may have forgotten is that being sexy is commended by God. In fact, God created us as sexual beings who en-

Our understanding of purity is based on God's holiness.

joy being admired sexually. It is the main reason we talk about modesty in how we dress.

Proverbs 5:19–Let her [your wife] be as the loving hind and pleasant roe; let her breasts satisfy thee at all times; and be thou ravished always with her love.

Can you imagine trying to apply this verse with a long-sleeve shirt that comes up high at the neck? Guess what? Wanting to be sexually appealing is okay. Notice though that this verse is talking about being sexy with just one person: your husband.

Hebrews 13:14a–Marriage is honorable in all, and the bed undefiled.

Being sensual is both appropriate and pure in this context. It is not sinful; rather, it is obeying God's Word!

Being sexy is a good thing, only in the right place: your bedroom. The Bible says that the *marriage bed* is undefiled (not sinful) and honorable (a good thing). God's way sounds like fun! Why do we assume if something is fun and pleasurable, it can't be from God?

God says that the right time to be sexy is in the context of marriage. When we are sexy in this time and place, sexiness is pure, holy, and fun. God's ways are always the best ways. If you are not married, you have to wait to be sexy *and* pure. Being sexy and pure can only happen in the context of marriage, according to the Bible.

Look at this picture again. Can a bikini be modest? What does the Bible say according to *Hebrews 13:14?* "Marriage is honorable in all, and the bed undefiled."

Can wearing a bikini be appropriate? Pure? Even *spiritual?* YES. As long as you are wearing it for your husband *alone* in *private*.

If we think about the definition of modesty and remember that purity is a big part of that definition, we will understand that being sensual in the right time and place with the right person is fun, guilt-free, and *modest*. BUT, being sensual in the wrong time and place and with the wrong person hurts us and those around us.

What if I'm not married?

These verses (*Proverbs 5:19, Hebrews 13:14*) explain why being sexy is okay in marriage. But why is being sexy a problem at other times? What if you are a long way from being married? Or what if you never get married?

Dressing sensually is a problem right now for several reasons. *First, being sexy communicates in public what should only be private: "Come and get me!"* It is an invitation for sexual intimacy. Is it hard to believe that what we wear says so much? The world knows our clothes communicate something about who we are, even if we Christians don't get it. See how a recent clothing catalog describes this concept. Notice how many of the verbs in these descriptions are communication words (Fall 2001 *Newport News Catalog*).

> These latest looks are body conscious without being self-conscious… they complement their wearer and encourage (in the wearing) a bit of sauciness in return. So, go on, paint your lips red, put a little swing in those hips, unleash that feisty sense of humor and embrace GLAMOUR!

> She's a little bit of sugar and a lot of spice, an irresistible combination of naughty and nice. She knows all about "packaging," dressing to make heads turn with sexy leathers and animal prints that emphasize her wild streak.

> She is, everyone agrees, the most feminine woman they know. She loves clothes that express her sensual side with passionate colors and decorative embellishments.

In fact, *TV Guide* editors demonstrated their understanding of the power of clothing when they interviewed a costume director a few years ago to show how a particular television series had changed significantly. Jill Ohanneson, costume designer for the television show *Roswell*, commented on the new personality of the show.

> We wanted to heighten the sexuality. For example, Liz has traded sweaters and skirts for cargo pants and tight T-shirts. She's working her way toward having sex with Max, so she's wearing more body-conscious things (October 6-12, 2001).

Notice that the clothing the characters wore were a significant part of "heightening the sexuality" and reaching a particular goal. Yes, the world knows sensual clothing is an invitation to intimacy.

2 *Second, dressing sensually outside the context of marriage can hurt our testimony.* Even unsaved people have expectations about what a Christian should wear. Did you know that even the world recognizes that short skirts are sensual? Business offices recognize what short skirts communicate. That is why the usual recommendation for business dress skirts is no more than one to two inches above the knee. These are not Christian companies making these guidelines. These secular companies recognize, though, that sexy clothing creates a sexy atmosphere, something desirable in the bed-room but not at work.

3 *Third, being sexy can cause good men to struggle and stumble.* God made men to want to admire a woman (their wife) sexually. This is a great thing when you are married because God also made women to enjoy being admired sexually. A godly man will want to save his sexual thoughts for his future wife. Do you want a godly man to avoid looking at you so that he can keep his thoughts pure?

4 *Fourth, being sexy in the wrong time and place hurts the treasure of a one-flesh marriage relationship.* It's too special to waste early, and it does affect your marriage.

That's not what I am say-ing when I dress this way!

Many girls who like to dress stylishly don't intend to be sensual: they just want to be in style or look attractive. Some styles are sexy though. These women are offended when a man makes a sexual comment or joke about them or to them. What they don't know is that even if their heart is right with God, what they wear still sends a message. What a Christian wears is important. Why? Because Christians are on display to the world as well as to other Christians. Look at these familiar verses.

Matthew 5:14- Ye are the light of the world.
A city that is set on a hill cannot be hid.

This verse shows how Christians are on display to the world. We cannot avoid being watched and evaluated by those unsaved people around us. What they think about us does matter.

Romans 14: 7, 16, 18- For none of us liveth to himself,
and no man dieth to himself. Let not then your good be evil
spoken of. For he that in these things serveth Christ is
acceptable to God, and approved of men.

These verses in Romans show that we are responsible for what we communicate to other believers, even if we don't intend to communicate those things. We also learn from these verses that good intentions don't erase our responsibility for how we are perceived.

 *1 Corinthians 13:1— Though I speak with the tongues of men and of angels, and have not charity, I am become as sounding brass, or a tinkling cymbal.*

Some women are selfish and don't care that what they wear causes men to struggle. They might be making a lot of obnoxious noise with their clothing, but they are not pleasing to God. Love for God and others is what keeps women from dressing in a way that does not protect the thoughts of Christian men around them. Love is also what influences many women to dress more conservatively than they otherwise would, even if they have the liberty to dress differently.

Shouldn't people avoid judging me based on what I wear?

Many women are bothered because people judge them by what they wear. They know that God sees their heart, but they forget that people can't see their heart: they see only the outside.

Because all people see of us is the outside, the outside of us is extremely important, as all of these verses show. Even if we do not intend to dress or act sensually, if that's what we are communicating, we are not being modest.

What is the big deal about skin anyway?

Why do you think it matters so much how much skin we show in public or how suggestive we are in how we dress? One important reason relates to how God made us as women.

When you see a magazine in the store with a beautiful woman on the cover, do you think of the woman's intelligence, sense of humor, or personality? Not often. In fact, this is why models often stress these qualities when they are interviewed by the media. Many models are actually quite accomplished and educated women; but when they show off their bodies, the public tends to view them as merely an object. This is one reason that wearing sexy clothing for all to see actually hurts them and us, when we do the same thing.

You are not a simple object; you are not merely a body. God made you into an incredibly complex person. He did not make you into a simple Barbie doll to be admired and played with. Furthermore, God's plan for the marriage relationship is that it beautifully illustrates our relationship with Him. Look at *Ephesians 5:31-32.* If you have ever had a longing to be cherished by someone, this longing is exactly what God wants us to have for Him.

If you have ever enjoyed or desired the closeness between a husband and wife, this desire is exactly what we are to desire for God and what He desires to have with us.

Remember that God created Adam and Eve for fellowship with Him! The world tends to deemphasize this intimacy of a biblical relationship. In doing so, they reduce a woman and physical intimacy to an object and an entertaining event. This is a degradation of God's creation and the illustration of our relationship with Him!

How else does the world de-emphasize intimacy? By emphasizing the physical part of a relationship as though that were all that mattered or was the most important part. For example, explicit movies focus on only one portion of a good relationship (not to mention they hurt the privacy and intimacy essential to a marriage relationship). Using street slang puts intimacy on the same level as a joke or a swear word. Gimmicky objects and clothes also put intimacy in a category of things to joke about. Sleazy gifts at wedding showers do the same de-emphasizing and should be avoided. Even as a joke, these gifts are inappropriate because they misrepresent the precious gift of intimacy that God gives to a husband and wife.

Building intimacy is a part of becoming one flesh, as God intended. Having secrets together that no one else knows builds this intimacy. Have you ever had a close friend tell someone else a secret you trusted her with? It's hard to trust that person with more secrets, isn't it? That's why you don't share details of your intimate life, including showing your body. Your body belongs to your husband. It is one of the most precious things you can give him. Because your body belongs to your husband (or will, if you are not married yet), do not share it with others. You are cultivating your husband's trust in you by being very careful not to reveal

While dressing in a way that reflects holiness and purity is great, some girls forget that modesty is more than just what they wear.

his secrets. *Proverbs 31:11* reminds us that the heart of the virtuous woman's husband trusts her completely. Having secrets, and knowing those secrets are safe between just the two of you, is a fun part of marriage. Those secrets help form a strong bond of friendship that is important in staying close.

While dressing in a way that reflects holiness and purity is important, some women forget that modesty is more than just what they wear. Much flirting is outside the bounds of appropriateness because it arouses the same sexual emotions that dressing provocatively does. This is why girls should refrain from touching boys, even in ways they may not perceive as sexual. They should avoid giving a friend that's a boy a massage or tickling him in fun. These types of touching are *immodest* until brought within the context of marriage.

Purity is also reflected in simple friendships. Especially as young people grow older, a close friendship between a guy and girl can be a stumblingblock for one or both of them. God designed us so that the closer a man and woman grow as friends, the more intimacy they create. He didn't design men and women to stay "just friends." Intimacy, especially for women, is difficult to separate into spiritual, emotional, or sexual categories. This is a wonderful part of being married! Praying together, sharing ideas together, and even laughing together develop a closeness that can further develop into a desire for sexual intimacy, which cannot be fulfilled biblically in an un-married couple. Both guys and girls must be careful in their friend-ships of the opposite sex. Being careful to think and act in a way that will prevent inappropriate behavior is a part of being pure, or modest. It is possible for a girl to be very careful to dress modestly but neglect to be careful to act modestly. A truly modest person will take care to think, act, and dress modestly.

How can I be pure in what I wear?

When in doubt, ask your husband, father, or godly older brother (not brother in Christ). Pay attention to what your dad and brothers say. Even if unsaved, they may have a perspective that is valuable. Even when we want to be modest, we ladies sometimes have difficulty understanding how we are perceived by our brothers in Christ.

Instead of asking an ungodly parent or husband, "Should I wear this?" or "Is this modest?" you may want to ask, "Is this outfit sexy or sensual?" or "Does this outfit draw attention to my breasts?" Then you can make a wise decision on whether the outfit is pleasing to the Lord in that particular context. (Unsaved and saved alike may agree that an outfit is sexy; they may differ on whether or not it is appropriate.)

If you have a large bust, it is especially important that you have a good bra. Check out Title Nine (www.title9.com) for a good selection of sports bras for ladies with a large bra size. If you are tall, look at J.C. Penney's (www.jcpenny.com) catalog specifically for tall women. You can also find a section on their website. Newport News (www.newport-news.com) has a large selection of stylish long skirts. Many of their other clothes are immodest, so be careful.

Does purity mean that I abandon femininity?

It is easy to complain that men can't understand about the trials of being a woman, but we forget that God made us different on purpose! Are you happy with how God made you?

Femininity is an attitude of contentment and delight in how God made us as women. When we enjoy who we are and how God made us, when we begin to understand how the inside of us works, then we can also choose clothing based on this principle of how God made us.

Feminine dress is simply clothing that is distinctly female. Now, before images of ruffles and lace go parading by in your mind, remember that ruffles and lace are by no means the only distinctly female qualities of clothing. Color, style, and fit all contribute to an overall feminine appearance. Yes, dresses are feminine (you won't see men wearing dresses very often); but other articles of clothing can be distinctly female as well. For example, it is possible to wear a suit that is a feminine color, with a rounded, small collar, and pretty buttons, making it distinctly different from the straight, angular cut of a man's business suit.

What about the command in *Deuteronomy 22:5* for women not to wear men's clothing and men not to wear women's clothing? While the command is to Israel and not the church, it nevertheless shows God's distaste for men and women who are discontent with their gender. When God gave this command, men's and women's dress was much different than our current clothing styles. Consequently it is unwise to be dogmatic in applying this verse to specific articles of clothing. Even though clothing in Bible times wasn't anything like American clothing today (a cultural difference), we can learn from this verse by identifying the principle that God was concerned about—that the distinction between men and women remain intact. A man trying to look like or act like a woman is a problem, but so is a woman who dresses to look like a man.

Because men and women do share items of clothing (white socks, for example, or pullover sweaters), it is wise to be careful that the overall style is clearly feminine or masculine. This care is pleasing to God. When wearing a gender-neutral article of clothing, look for small details that make it distinctly feminine. For example, a plaid flannel shirt can look quite masculine unless the fit or color makes it distinctively female. What about a baseball cap? Have you seen a girl wear a cap in such a way that it is difficult to tell that she's a girl?

Of course, femininity is more than just wearing feminine clothes, just as modesty is more than wearing modest clothes. Sometimes, women take part in activities that are not identified as distinctly feminine. What about hunting or backpacking? Playing paintball? Shooting a gun? Does embracing femininity mean that a young woman must reject these activities and instead embroider pillows all her life?

A feminine woman is characterized by contentment with who God made her to be.

If we can enjoy how God made us, it can be a fun challenge to bring a feminine style to activities like these. A lot of being feminine is not what you do but how you do it. For example, a girl doesn't have to bring a cordless curling iron along on a backpacking trip, but she may decide to wash her hair and brush her teeth along the way.

Having an opinion is not a problem, but the manner of giving it may be. A feminine woman will not walk like a man (or elephant) or talk loudly and pound a table to get across her point. She will not focus on trying to do everything a man can do. She will not choose activities merely to prove a point or to be with the guys. Her life will be characterized by contentment with who God made her to be.

A married woman chooses to be feminine when she works on following her husband's leadership. Many women expect their husbands to be expert leaders without paying attention to the difficulty of learning to follow. She encourages him to lead by asking his opinion, by changing her priorities to his priorities as the leader of the household, and by enjoying the work God has called her to do.

Developing a feminine style is easier for some women than others. It is a quality that is cultivated, not an article of clothing that you put on. Like Paul, many women must *learn* to be content *(Philippians 4:11)* with how God made them. Because femininity is an inside characteristic (how we think) that finds its way outside in how we act and dress, femininity is something we can grow into.

4

Modesty is Appropriate

When the Apostle Paul commanded Timothy to teach the women in his church to dress modestly, he was talking largely about dressing appropriately. This principle affects many clothing choices that may not be problematic in any other way. Your ability to choose clothing that fits the situation or occasion is an essential part of being modest. An outfit may in fact fit all of the other criteria we have looked at and still not be acceptable.

A modest woman seeks to be appropriate by choosing clothing that fits the situation.

Would you wear a clown outfit to attend a funeral or a wedding? Would you wear old work clothes to visit someone important? Wearing clothes that fit the occasion shows respect for those people to whom we are ministering. This is why many Christians dress up when they go to church. They dress up to honor the Lord, much the same way that you may dress up to go visit an important person like the President's wife.

Taking the time to find out what kind of dress is expected at an event can save you and others from being embarrassed or uncomfortable. If you were going to the house of someone who visited your church and they happened to be very poor, would you dress in your finest dressy clothes, complete with sparkly jewels and designer shoes? A modest woman will consider to whom she is ministering when she chooses what she will wear.

Likewise, a teen may wear a white shirt to a church carwash. Because white t-shirts often become rather transparent when they get wet, what may be perfectly acceptable in any other situation is *not* acceptable at a car wash. It is inappropriate and therefore immodest. A skirt that is perfectly appropriate for wearing to the grocery store may be quite immodest hiking up a steep mountain trail. Likewise, what a young woman may choose to wear in the privacy of a dorm room may not be appropriate in public.

It is often the situation that determines modesty.

A modest woman seeks to be appropriate by choosing clothes that reflect her love for other believers.

If you want to serve God, but wear clothes others see as a problem, you may find that the influence you have on others is limited because you are giving mixed signals: what you wear appears to contradict what you say. Even if people wrongly judge your motives and heart, you still will lose some influence you might have had. If you are aware that what you wear poses a problem for another believer, it is especially good and commendable to avoid wearing that type of clothing in his presence. One singing group from a Christian college went to Eastern Europe for a singing tour. The clothing the ladies from this group wore was deliberately simple with somewhat darker colors, and the ladies did not wear makeup or jewelry. Why? Because the college believed those things were spiritual? No, because in the culture they were trying to minister to, wearing bright colors and makeup would have interfered with the ministry these young people wanted to have to the believers in this country. These young ladies did not complain, because they were excited about ministering to others. The love they had for these believers in another country prevented them from feeling irritated at the changes they had to make in their dress.

Instead of criticizing or complaining because somebody holds a different standard than you, consider how what you wear can show your love for that person or group of people. Girls who selfishly wear what pleases themselves, regardless of its effect on other believers, show a remarkable lack of love for their brothers and sisters in Christ. This is what Paul is talking about when he instructs the Philippian

It is love that will influence a young lady to avoid clothing that is not a problem in her eyes but that is in others' eyes.

church to "look not every man on his own things, but every man also on the things of others" *(Philippians 2:4).* Part of the definition of love given in *1 Corinthians 13* is that love "seeketh not her own." It really doesn't matter who is "right" about what is modest; selfishly holding a position is immodest anyway.

Married women can show love in what they wear by dressing in a way that pleases their husbands. Many ladies spend hours getting ready to go out in public but spend little or no time to look nice for their husbands when they come home from work. Take the time to get your husband's opinion on clothes that you wear in public. If you have differing tastes, try to find clothes that you both like. These are loving actions that consider your husband's desires above your own *(Philippians 2).*

A modest woman seeks to be appropriate by choosing clothes that are understood within her culture (environment) as modest.

Some Christians disagree on the role our culture plays in our clothing choices. Many believe that culture alone determines whether clothing is modest or not. They point out that ankles were considered to be immodest one hundred years ago, yet today even the most careful Christian woman among us isn't likely to hide her ankles because she thinks they are sexy. This reasoning is often used to demonstrate that a particular clothing standard is unreasonable because it is based on a cultural trend now obsolete. Sometimes people also use this argument to disprove the idea that clothing can be inherently immodest.

God does have a standard of clothing in the Bible.

The problem with this position is that it seems to overlook the fact that God *does* have a standard of clothing in the Bible. When Adam and Eve sinned, their consciences alone drove them to cover themselves. God then replaced their insufficient clothing to cover their nakedness. Have you ever wondered what God covered? It is likely that he covered the parts of a person that make them distinctly male or female. After the fall, public nakedness (and even partial nakedness) became associated with shame, perhaps because it became difficult to separate a person's nakedness from sinful thoughts and actions associated with nakedness. (For examples, see *Exodus 32:25*, *Isaiah 47:3*, and *Revelation 16:15*.) We cannot come to a conclusion as to what to wear simply because a standard exists that is not affected by our particular culture. We need discernment in understanding how today's clothing honors God's standard that He established in the Garden of Eden.

Although it is clear that culture does not by itself determine modesty, it is nevertheless important to examine the role of culture in our clothing choices. First, societal norms do affect modesty. A hundred years ago, it would have been inappropriate to show your ankles because the culture as a whole perceived this as inappropriately sexy. If a lady wanted to have a good testimony for the Lord, she would avoid doing something that would be perceived as inappropriate by those she desired to influence. Likewise, a believer today should be aware of how her clothing is perceived by others and with discernment, choose clothing that will allow her the greatest testimony.

Societal perceptions do change, and so will our clothing styles. We do not continue to wear bustled floor-length skirts today because they do not communicate sensibility in our American culture. Try suggesting to your pastor's wife that you want to emulate Rebekah's example in the Bible, including her nose ring *(Genesis 24:47)*. It is likely that your nose ring would be perceived as inappropriate by your employer or in your church today, even though it was not inappropriate in Bible times. Whereas a nose ring in Rebekah's world would not have been noticed, it would immediately draw attention in our world today and consequently express an attitude unbecoming of a modest Christian woman. Because of changes like these, we must continually re-evaluate our clothing in light of what it communicates within the world—to unbelievers as well as believers.

When a culture associates a particular clothing style with behavior or motivations that are sinful for a Christian, it must be rejected. For instance, in some Asian countries, a sleeveless blouse identifies a woman as a prostitute, even in seasons of sweltering heat. A Christian missionary living there would mar her testimony and greatly diminish her ability to communicate the gospel effectively if she ignored this fact and wore even the most modest sleeveless blouse. In another country, a diamond wedding ring is associated with extreme materialism and communicates a gaudy display of arrogance. Missionaries wishing to make friends and influence others in this country would find themselves regarded with disdain if they wore rings that even the poor in America commonly wear.

Remember that even if an article of clothing has no negative cultural connotation for you, others around you may still have those associations. Several genuinely godly college-age ladies were surprised to find out that their shoes and fishnet hose that they thought were beautiful and modest were actually considered highly inappropriate by a number of older folks, including their unsaved employers. The problem was that these items of clothing were associated with prostitution for many years, and this association was still very real to people to whom these girls wanted to minister. What would you have done in this situation? How would love play a role in your decision?

Obedience to God takes precedence over the opinions of society.

We should not violate clear biblical principles in order to be "culturally relevant." If it becomes appropriate within our pagan society to go topless in public, we should not adapt our clothing style to accommodate this perversion. While the Bible plainly expects us to consider those around us as we determine how we act, the Bible is also clear that obedience to God takes precedence over the opinions of society. So then, although cultural norms do *influence* what you wear, they should not by themselves *determine* what you wear.

A modest woman seeks to be appropriate by choosing clothes that fit the letter and spirit of the guidelines her authority sets up.

Ideally, all guidelines in our lives should have a clear biblical rationale or be based on principles found in the Bible. Sometimes a young woman may find herself in the position of not understanding or agreeing with these reasons. Occasionally, she will not be able to find any reason at all for the standards placed upon her. In these situations, it is helpful to remember that ultimately, whether a young woman agrees with or understands a clothing rule matters very little as long as she is under that authority. For example, God does not say anything about whether purple socks are sinful. Suppose, though, that purple socks were against the school/work rules. A girl may say to herself, "Well, since there's nothing in the Bible about purple socks, I'm going to wear them anyway." She may be correct, that there's really nothing wrong with wearing purple socks; however, for her, wearing purple socks would be sinful, because God has very clearly told us to submit to the authority He gives us.

If you struggle with a clothing rule, (like not being allowed to wear purple socks), the root issue for you is no longer about modesty. Instead, it is about submitting to authority, something a modest woman will seek to do. God can use situations like these to reveal your commitment to submitting to authority.

On the other hand, if an outfit you put on is clearly immodest even if it fits the rules, it is wrong to wear it. Remember, modesty is about pleasing God, not pleasing man. Wearing an immodest outfit in this situation is not truly respecting and submitting to the authority God has placed us under. Of course, we do not submit to authority that is clearly outside the bounds of God's Word. If you are a waitress and your boss wants you to wear a low-cut blouse to show some cleavage, that violates a biblical standard of modesty. In this situation, you should seek to appeal rather than helplessly follow the rules. Remember that God's principles hold precedence over man's rules.

God's principles hold precedence over man's rules.

Don't get trapped into following the rules without understanding why they exist. Seek as best you can to understand the reasons for the standards in your home, school, or church. You'll have far more fun with modesty if you know why you do what you do. But remember, how you seek to find answers (tone of voice, respect for authority, and facial expressions) can be done immodestly too.

Are you growing in your understanding of what it means to please God with a heart attitude of modesty? Does the challenge of living modestly seem overwhelming sometimes? It is a great encouragement to me as I look at how far I have to go to be Christlike, that God's mercy also extends endlessly. Remember that learning and applying these truths will take a lifetime! Martin Luther correctly stated that Christian growth is more important than Christian achievement. Modesty takes work; and around every corner of growth, we will find new ways of using our knowledge of God's plan for us as women. God designed our Christian walk to be satisfying and joyful. I pray that your journey is every bit what God intended it to be.

This life therefore, is not Righteousness, but growth
in righteousness, not health but healing, not being
but becoming, not rest but exercise. We are not yet
what we shall be, but we are growing toward it;
the process is not yet finished but it is going on.
This is not the end of the road; all does not yet
gleam in glory but all is being purified.

Martin Luther

Appendix 1

Specific Help in
Dressing Modestly

Now that we have discussed when we can be sexy, it will be helpful to discuss specific ways that we can be, or not be, sexy. You probably know some of this material already; but because there are some issues that are either confusing or unclear, ladies often misunderstand these important concepts of dressing modestly.

If you are not married, consider the following discussion instructional. Some parts of the discussion will be obvious to you. Other parts might make you stop to think. In any case, when you know you want to be sexy for your husband, it is important that you know how to do it right! Don't worry, it's worth the wait! When you are married and experience God's plan for intimacy, you will gain tremendous understanding of the principles you have applied in faith.

If you are married, you may find this discussion makes more sense to you than to an unmarried sister in Christ. That is because you have experienced the intimacy that is integral to developing a pure and holy modesty. You may find the material gives you more understanding of concepts you may have known intuitively. For you, dressing and being sexy is a great option for private times with your husband (still off limits biblically in public).

Let's review our definition of sexy. A simple way to think of it is that being sexy is to draw attention to sexual parts of your body, typically a woman's breasts or bottom. You already knew that, didn't you? Clothing that accomplishes this purpose is called sensual. Look at how the dictionary defines *sensual*: "Providing gratification [or satisfying] of the physical and especially the sexual appetite; suggesting sexuality" (AHD 4th edition). Remember, as wives this is exactly what we want to accomplish for our husbands. Sensuality is great when we keep it in the right context. God designed husbands and wives to satisfy each other sexually. To the extent that sexy clothing accomplishes this goal in its proper context, the clothing itself can be wonderfully pure.

How covering skin can be immodest

The next important lesson to learn is that you don't have to reveal your body to draw attention to it. All you have to do is make a suggestion. The world knows this. Why do you think lingerie stores stay in business? Why wear anything at all?

Clothing manufacturers understand this concept, too, and use it to their advantage. One season, the shirts are loose-fitting, but the skirts are short. The next season, the skirts are long but have huge slits up to the thigh. Maybe the next season, all the tops will be clingy. Typically, each season, some part of the in-style fashion will intentionally draw attention to some sexual part of the body: a woman's breasts, her legs, her rear, and so on. The only trouble is these styles are designed to be worn in public, and a modest woman wants to be sexy in private. So she will avoid being manipulated by the clothing manufacturers' strategy.

A modest woman wants to be sexy in private.

Lucky Jeans makes money on the suggestive quality of sexuality. Their jeans say "lucky you" on the fly. Why do you think those words are there? They are not on the outside. The suggestion of sexuality is all they need to successfully market their clothing. Clothing designers generally use more common strategies to create the suggestion of sensuality. Clingy and sheer can clearly be suggestive. You can't see everything, but you can see something. The clothing "teases" by giving a little view but not the whole thing. One way that you know it is an effective strategy is that it sells clothes. Clothing manufacturers don't really care what you look like; they will ultimately sell what makes them money.

Because teenagers often wear tight shirts, shirts marketed to teens are tighter and smaller than they would be if they were marketed to older women. In this case, if you are a teenager, you will either have to buy a bigger size than you normally would or just look for shirts outside the teenager department. Don't worry about expanding your shopping domain. You may be surprised to find clothing that you like in other areas of the store, even if you may not ever wear everything in those sections. Typically, stores that cater to teenagers do not carry many classic styles.

Showing cleavage is considered suggestive. You don't have to go topless to show off your breasts. A low neckline is sexy. So is a tight t-shirt. When you find a t-shirt that is too tight, it's okay to buy a bigger size. I recently went shopping for a casual t-shirt. I found one I liked and bought it, all the time with a niggling thought in my mind that the large would be the best size, even though I've always worn a small or medium. I was in a hurry, so I just grabbed the medium, paid for it, and took it home. Do you know that when I got home the medium was too tight? It wasn't extremely tight, but just enough to make me uncomfortable. When I exchanged the medium for the large, I was amazed at how much better it looked and was happy I had made the right choice even though it was difficult. I had to remind myself that large doesn't mean fat.

How can you decide if your clothing is too tight? One way is to evaluate how much slack a garment has on your body. Clothing ranges from ultra tight, with no fabric slack, to extremely loose and baggy. It is better to buy clothes that are not perfectly form-fitting (like tight jeans or shirts that cling to the bottom of your breasts). These tight styles can draw attention to a woman's body in an inappropriate way.

Not as obviously suggestive is a dramatic slit. While slits are often functional (walking may be quite difficult if you sew them completely), they also can be suggestive. The long slits on glamour dresses are obviously not there just so the wearer can walk more easily. Sometimes it is difficult to tell the difference between a functional slit and a suggestive one. Some Christian ladies avoid the problem by avoiding slits altogether or sewing the slits closed. This can be a great strategy of your own as long as you have skirts that you can walk in after you sew up the slits! This strategy may be appropriate for some skirt styles and not others. Seek a second opinion from your husband or trusted friend in determining what would be a modest approach in this area.

A modest woman goes out of her way to be pure and appropriate in all areas of life, not just in dress. Here are ways she does this.

 She doesn't casually discuss topics like her monthly cycle in mixed company. For the most part, the guys around us should never know we are in the midst of our cycle.

 She is uncomfortable mentioning body parts in public. Most girls would be uncomfortable yelling across a table, "My breasts are sore!" and at the same time are comfortable yelling across a table, "Get your butt over here" or "I gotta go pee." There's not much difference.

3 She is uncomfortable with sitcoms and movies that discuss private topics as humor or casual conversation. Intimacy is far more precious than that!

 4 She is aware of her body and how it can be seen. This awareness can prevent her from being immodest unintentionally. In the context of marriage, this awareness can help her to be very sexy.

Unintentional Immodesty

Can a person be immodest without realizing it? Yes! While some girls struggle with wanting to wear sexy clothes in public, many girls don't. They sincerely want to be modest and pure in all areas of their lives. They buy clothing because it is cute, their friends think it is cute, or it is "normal" and they don't think about it. Because dressing sexy is the furthest thing from their minds, they have a hard time understanding how their clothing could be interpreted as sexy. They may also have a hard time trusting a teacher who tells them that their clothing is inappropriate.

When they look in the mirror, they are standing up straight. Throughout the day, they are bending, leaning, sitting—all actions that can be immodest in an outfit that looked okay in the mirror that morning. So, when you look in the mirror, be sure to bend over, reach your arms up, and sit down on a chair to fully "test" the appropriateness of your clothing.

Remember, too, that different bodies have different problems. If a woman looks at her friends to see how clothing looks, but her friends have a different body shape, she could be misled into thinking the same clothing is okay for her too. Women with an ample bust line have to be far more aware of their necklines and gaping between blouse buttons. Some clothing styles may be impossible for her to wear modestly. Women with a small bust line simply don't have these problems but still need to wear lined bras that properly pad her breasts.

Likewise, a short woman wearing a skirt that comes to the top of her knees looks different than a tall woman wearing a skirt that comes to the top of her knees. A tall woman can look quite sexy following the same rule that the short woman is following but without the same effect.

This is why girls and women can follow school, church, or work guidelines and look completely different. This is also why rules are helpful guidelines, but they do not determine modesty. There is nothing sacred about the knee. Women should follow these guidelines; but if what they wear fits the rules and is still not modest, they should not wear it.

Be aware of how you sit, too. Keeping your legs together isn't just something that older ladies taught girls in charm school. Girls sometimes have difficulty remembering that they must sit differently in a skirt than they do in a pair of jeans. A girl in a skirt who sits with her legs wide apart can give a very good view of her pretty underwear and can be a distraction if she is sitting across from others (e.g., in a gym, in the front rows of class or church, among a round circle of chairs). So be careful!

Rules are helpful guidelines, but they do not determine modesty.

Try an experiment. Wear a skirt that has a front or side slit in it, and see how high it goes when you sit down. A slit that comes to the bend of the knee when you stand might be past your thigh, and therefore showing too much leg, when you sit down. Being aware of this problem before you wear the skirt in public is helpful, since you can adjust the slit so it doesn't show too much. You may find, though, that you don't like worrying about your slit, especially if you're sitting all day, and decide to just not wear it.

Sleeveless shirts can cause problems when the armhole is large enough to reveal your bra to someone standing next to you. Check in the mirror, moving your arm to see.

Sheer white blouses are usually something older ladies often have trouble with. These blouses unknowingly give people behind (and in front of) them a view of their underwear. These ladies often wear a camisole, but then they're showing off a not-so-attractive view of both the bra and the camisole. Unless the camisole or undershirt you're wearing really does cover your bra and doesn't look like underwear, avoid wearing these white shirts. Look hard for white shirts that are lined or of a thicker material that won't be so sheer. Look for a camisole with wide straps that actually cover the bra straps instead of adding a second pair. Or reserve the sheer blouses for under blazers that cover these questionable areas. Lastly, remember that white becomes more sheer when wet, so think twice about the activity you are attending to make sure the shirt is appropriate.

Although bra straps aren't really sexy, they do draw attention to your underwear and indirectly to your breasts. We should be uncomfortable anytime our underwear is noticeable. Interestingly enough, some people have decided that bra straps are an asset and are selling decorated replacement straps. Whether intentional or not, exposed bra straps are not appropriate.

Remember that your breasts change when they are cold or you are under stress. You may find that although your bra had good coverage when you first put on your clothes, going outside to the car could cause problems! Save your thin, attractive bras for when you are wearing a top that is loose, bulky, or has a busy pattern. You don't want your nipples to show through your clothes. Make sure you have at least one good bra that doesn't show your nipples, no matter how cold you are. If you're having difficulty finding something, ask a sales clerk at a department store to recommend a "seamless bra with good coverage." She'll help you out.

You also want to be careful wearing underwear that shows through your clothing. Skirts or pants that are too tight may show your underwear, and some sheer fabrics show your underwear even if your clothing is not too tight. Bikini and thong-style underwear tends to show through these styles and be quite distracting. If you like these styles and they are comfortable for you, make sure you have a few pairs of solid, light-colored, brief-style underwear for when you need something that won't show through.

Ultimately you may find an outfit that is too distracting to wear. If you will spend more than once or twice in the day checking your neckline or length, decide the outfit isn't worth the fuss. You will be much more comfortable if you're not worrying about whether something is showing. This isn't necessarily a sin issue; it's just common sense.

Modesty is Consistent

Some girls who are concerned about being modest are not consistent when they look for a wedding dress. They may wear a dress with a neckline they would never wear in another situation. Why? Usually because many wedding dresses have low necklines or other problems. It can be difficult to find one that they like and one that is modest.

What can you do? Find a seamstress who can fix the dress. A good seamstress can often raise necklines or even change an off-the-shoulder gown into a gown with capped sleeves. The work to make your wedding dress modest is worth it. You don't want to be uncomfortable on your wedding day because you're not used to so much skin showing.

Consistency is important in other areas. A friend of mine wasn't allowed to wear a miniskirt when she was a teen. She asked her mom why, since she was allowed to wear a bikini to the beach. "Skin is skin," she told her mom. You know, she was right! You can buy very lovely underwear, but most people would feel uncomfortable going shopping wearing only that underwear. Where you are doesn't change much, whether it's on the beach or walking down a wedding aisle.

Appendix 2

Thoughts for the Teacher of Modesty

1 *Teach modesty as a positive attribute.* Many modesty discussions are primarily negative: don't dress this way, period. These talks often neglect to explain the positive: there's a very good reason we don't dress or act a certain way. Starting with the negative can put even girls who want to do right on the defensive! As one author says, "Parents must teach their children to consider *tznius (Heb. Modesty)* a delightful and admirable way of dress, and *pritzus (Heb. Immodesty)* as something deplorable and shameful.... [If] she does not get the impression that *tznius* is delightful and *pritzus* degrading and shameful, but rather thinks that the former is merely 'good conduct' and the latter just a 'wrongdoing' she will not develop a love and admiration for *tznius*" (*Modesty: An Adornment for Life* Falk, 181). As David says, "O taste and see that the Lord is good!" *(Psalm 34:8).* This is the exuberant attitude we must convey.

2 *Teach girls how to apply biblical principles to their dress.* Learning to apply biblical principles isn't as "safe" as giving a list of rules. Rules are so often attractive to us Christians because they can give the appearance of spirituality while, in fact, providing an escape from the much more difficult duty of teaching believers to carefully think through a complex issue, in principle, and then think through responsible application which honors Christ. Sometimes a woman will sincerely apply the same Word of God that you do and wear something you believe is inappropriate. When this happens, do not be distressed or alarmed. The same Holy Spirit working in your life is working in her life, if she is a believer.

Careless criticism may discourage a sincere desire to apply the Bible. Instead, be thankful that this child of God is seeking to apply the Bible to her life, and trust the Lord to guide her as she applies the principles she has been taught. Many never reach this level of maturity. If you decide that it is appropriate to discuss this woman's dress with her, be as patient and as gracious as you would want others to be with you. Consider that God does not correct us every time we misunderstand or mis-apply the Bible.

3   *Remember that the application of modesty may change with our bodies.* As our bodies change, changes in dress may be required to adhere to the principles of modesty. Women gain and lose weight, and outfits that may have been modest when first purchased may not be modest some time later. Even a woman committed to

modesty may in this way occasionally wear an outfit she is uncomfortable with.

Young girls whose bodies are changing often do not realize that the t-shirts they've been wearing without any problem suddenly become too tight or revealing. They may find that skirts that were once long enough may get shorter with a growth spurt.

When I became pregnant, my changing body shape gave me much insight all over again into dressing modestly. The challenge of finding maternity clothes that I liked and that were also modest was tremendous. It reminded me that many teens have a similar difficulty finding clothes they like but that are still modest and within a price budget.

When I began nursing my first child, I experienced for the first time the discouragement others have of trying to find clothes that are not too tight on top but that still fit everywhere else. The nursing bras I bought didn't provide good coverage like I was used to, and I had several humbling moments when I realized that I had been one of the "immodest" ladies that girls are warned about.

Because our bodies change, like it or not, as we age, we must be careful that we do not communicate the idea that modesty is something that we achieve and never have to consider again after we obtain a "modest" wardrobe. Emphasize to your students, counselees, or daughters that modesty is a *lifestyle* that needs periodic reevaluation. Help them to be thankful for parents, husbands, authority, mentors, and peers who challenge us to reevaluate and change when there is a need.

4 Refuse to criticize women who choose to wear/not wear certain articles of clothing because they believe this pleases the Lord Being critical of another believer's sincere desire to please the Lord does not cultivate the unity that is so important to the body of Christ. Although you may disagree with the choices some women have made, endeavor to keep the unity of the Spirit in the bond of peace *(Ephesians 4:3).* Look for an opportunity to humbly correct an unbiblical position according to the Scripture, or even simply to give your opinion if asked. In this case, consider carefully Jesus' cautions in *Matthew 7:1-2* to examine our own hearts before confronting another.

It is sometimes fashionable to ridicule those standards that seem to us to be excessive or inadequate. Mocking another's dress is never acceptable for a Christian in any case, but making fun of a decision sincerely made for spiritual reasons is reprehensible. This behavior is evidence of pride, something God clearly states is an abomination to Him *(Proverbs 6:16-17)*. As a teacher, mentor, or mother, you must set a good example for your girls and make clear your expectations of humility in allowing these differences. Do not allow them to make fun of others or be critical of others. Set an example of Christian charity to those who hold positions that may be more conservative or less conservative than your own position.

On the other hand, recognize that even women who desire to please the Lord and are committed to biblical modesty may occasionally wear an outfit that makes you cringe. Be patient with others, and in love give them the benefit of the doubt *(1 Corinthians 13:7)*. A *pattern* of immodesty is different than a single occasion of "borderline dress." Sometimes a woman may not realize an outfit is inappropriate until it is too late to do something about it. I have been in the middle of church and had my husband lean over and say to me something like, "You know, your blouse needs a camisole." In times like these, I am thankful for the graciousness of other believers who do not write me off for a single incident.

5. *Be honest about issues that do not have a clear biblical basis.* As teachers, we need to be careful to use Scripture when we say we are using a biblical position. Sometimes we may not have a specific biblical position but just don't feel comfortable with what a girl is wearing. One approach would be to acknowledge that the rule in question is indeed subjective. Explain that it can only be "justified" as a parental / authority effort to provide what we hope the Lord will bless as a "wisdom" rule for the protection of our children. Remind them that the only way we can discover if the Holy Spirit has, in truth, granted us a submissive heart is if we submit when we *don't* agree. When we agree with a rule, submission is not needed. It may be wise to agree to pray that the Lord will show you if the rule is indeed unreasonable or irrelevant. Agree that if God shows you that this is the case, you will be willing to remove the questioned rule. Changing a rule does not necessarily mean that you were sinning to have the rule or that you are sinning to change it. Sanctification is a continual process from which none of us is exempt.

6 *Ultimately, remember that no modesty lecture or discussion can change a woman's heart.* Recognize that although we need to be patient in waiting for the Holy Spirit to work in others' lives, they may never change to meet our standards of modesty. This does not necessarily mean they are being rebellious or are unsaved. Only the Holy Spirit can change a heart, and His timetable may be different than ours. Our responsibility is to give the truth of God's Word in love and then let God be God. In faith, believe His promise that His Word will not return void.

Appendix 3

Thoughts for
Mothers and Fathers

What is beautiful to you may not be beautiful to your daughter. To a certain degree, the differences between people's tastes are personality differences. I have two nephews: one nephew at age six loved wild prints and bright colors. The other at age nine would have been mortified to be caught wearing a Hawaiian print shirt. Instead, he tried to stick with neutral colors that did not stand out. Even at a young age, their choices in clothing reflected their personalities. I am thankful that their mother did not try to fit them into a particular mold. It is important if you are a mother that you respect the choices of your children. If you like conservative, classic colors and you have a daughter who loves high-contrast colors, you will find more success buying clothes that reflect her tastes, not yours. Of course, it is never right to go into debt trying to please your children's clothing styles.

Until your daughters demonstrate maturity and discernment in purchasing clothes, consider shopping with your daughter for all of her clothes. It is much easier to put back unsuitable clothing than it is to take it back once the clothing is purchased and brought home. While shopping, instead of always identifying problems with clothes, encourage your daughter to evaluate what she likes. Ask questions, try things on for size, and do not jump to conclusions or lose your composure if she looks at things that are obviously immodest. Ask, "What do you think about this? Do you like it?"

Consider purchasing all the basic clothing for your daughter instead of requiring her to buy it all herself. The pressure to find clothes on a very small budget can lead teenagers to purchase clothes at inexpensive teenager stores with very little modest selections. Cheaper bras often do not fit well or provide good coverage. While many department stores have semiannual lingerie sales which keep the costs lower, the bras there will still be more expensive than the bras found in discount stores. Paying for these basics will ensure that your daughter has what she needs.

One mother with several girls put bras that her older daughters had outgrown and new bras she had purchased on sale in a bag in her closet. Her girls could then find a bra that fit, without the embarrassment of shopping for a bigger size. Another mother bought a training bra for her daughter before she needed it. She then handed it to her daughter in a brown bag without any comment. Several months later, the girl finally got up enough courage to wear it in public. Contrast this example with a mother who fought with her daughter over wearing a bra because the daughter thought people would notice it. Sometimes taking your daughter to be fitted at a department store is the best option. Use discernment.

Consider helping your daughter find makeup that looks good on her. Some cheap makeup (such as the kind that teenagers with limited cash often buy) doesn't blend in well with the face, drawing more attention to the makeup instead of the face. The problem is not too much makeup but cheap makeup. Often, more expensive makeup will look more natural, because the ingredients used are of higher quality. Also know the target age for a makeup company; for example, Merle Norman makeup is designed for older women: it tends to be thicker and less sheer than other brands.

Look for ways to fix unacceptable clothes. You may be able to buy some coordinating fabric to insert into a neckline that is too low, and you may be able to pull up a neckline by adjusting the shoulder seams. If you can fix it without anyone knowing the difference, then it is worth fixing. If you cannot sew, consider having the outfit altered by someone else. Many dry cleaners also alter clothing for reasonable prices. If your daughter doesn't like it, don't force her to wear it, even if it is modest.

Don't wait until right before you leave for church, a fancy banquet, or somewhere else to evaluate a new outfit. If the clothing is inappropriate, the process of identifying the error and changing the clothing in question during a high-pressure time can be traumatic. Preventing this problem by checking an outfit ahead of time is a simple and loving measure.

Take the time to learn and teach what kinds of colors and styles look good on your daughter. If you start young and give her a framework from which to evaluate clothes on herself, she will be less likely to depend on the advice of others to evaluate her clothes.

Make sure that your relationship with your husband is right. Ask for his opinion of what *you* wear, and listen! Find clothing that you both like. I am surprised by how many women disregard their husband's opinion about simple taste (I like that, or I don't like that) and modesty. Furthermore, many mothers communicate by their words and actions that Dad is an ignorant dufus when it comes to appearance. A lack of respect for a husband's opinion sets a bad precedent for the daughters to likewise ignore both Mom and Dad's opinions on clothing, and later on, the daughter's own husband.

A family's understanding of modesty benefits from both a husband and a wife's contribution. Both must be willing to learn from each other and not be dismayed when a spouse lacks understanding. Children quickly perceive parental disagreement on family guidelines and naturally exploit these differences when it is to their advantage to do so. For this reason, it is best if parents can come to an acceptable agreement on family policies that both are willing to wholeheartedly support. Then, in a united front, they are able to give their children a biblical rationale for these policies.

Understand that immodest dress can be a symptom of a spiritual problem rather than the problem itself. In these cases, repeatedly addressing the problem with modesty is unlikely to correct the problem and may actually hide the problem if a daughter yields to pressure to change her clothing without changing her heart. In these cases, it is better to focus on having a vibrant relationship with the Lord and keep clothing lectures to a minimum. As a young lady learns to walk in the Spirit, her behavior and dress will reflect the heart change.

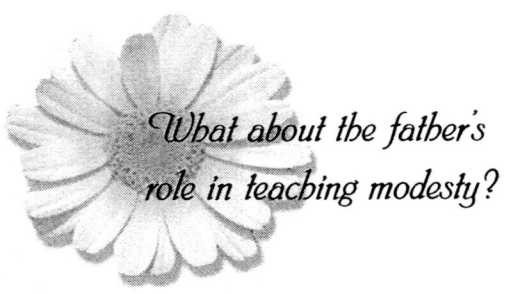
What about the father's role in teaching modesty?

While the mother is the primary instructor (my husband calls her the sergeant), the dad is the general. In the military, the general has responsibility for the jobs getting done; he provides materiel support (in our case, money to buy clothes!) and encouragement for his staff, but he doesn't attend to every detail.

We often think of Dad's role being bigger in confrontation: "You're not going out of the house wearing THAT," or even telling his wife he does not want her buying immodest clothes for the daughter. (If the sergeant won't listen to the general, you have an authority problem, not a modesty problem. All the modesty discussions in the world will not change anything in this situation.) Actually, confrontation should rarely be necessary.

Dad's role also comes to play when his daughters are not rebelling: having a close relationship with them is essential. It begins by admiring them when they are little girls, not only for their beauty but also for their modest clothes and modest attitudes. Dad is the one who communicates to his little girl that modesty is beautiful, regal (like a queen or princess), and admirable. When Dad communicates that modesty is something to be admired and that immodesty is beneath the dignity of a lady, he will go a lot further than the modesty-is-good, immodesty-is-sinful model. There's a subtle but significant difference.

He should be willing to give feedback as it is asked for. Dad's attitude toward Mom and how she dresses is also important. Does he complain if she spends "too much money" for a beautiful and modest dress? (I know some women can go out of control when it comes to spending, but some dads are unrealistic when it comes to clothing costs.) Does he admire her in front of the family?

It is very helpful for dads to be willing to go shopping with or for the women in his household or simply supply money for shopping. I remember very clearly as a young teen when one time my dad commented on an outfit of mine that he didn't like. I asked him to help me find me a dress he did like. By the end of the week, I had a new dress that we both liked, and I didn't wear the old outfit. The fact that my dad was willing to share in the chore of finding appropriate clothes meant a lot to me.

Taking the time to help a daughter shop gives a dad insight into the challenge of maintaining modesty. It can help him be compassionate and patient as his daughters mature into modest women of God.

Application 1

Defining Modesty

Write here a good definition of modesty in your own words. Remember that we get definitions for biblical concepts from Scripture, not necessarily from the dictionary or books, including this book. Use the Scripture verses given in the text (and any other verses you can think of) to help.

_____

_____

_____

The first important part of the biblical definition is that modesty is not what you wear. Modesty is not a "good" article of clothing, and immodesty is not a "bad" article of clothing. The Bible tells us that modesty is quite different. Modesty is what you are, not what you wear.

What do you think this paragraph means? Give an example.

_____

_____

_____

Describe a biblically modest teenager. Make sure you discuss how she thinks and acts as well as how she dresses.

_____

_____

_____

_____

_____

Do you have a desire to be like the person you just described? Why or why not?

_____

_____

_____

_____

Application 2

Fashion Scavenger Hunt

For the following activity, provide a variety of clothing catalogs, demonstrating both modest and immodest clothing. Below are a few suggestions. You can order catalogs from the websites, or you can go to a mall and pick up catalogs at individual stores. Some you may need to purchase. You may also challenge your students or counselees to bring in catalogs of stores where teenagers like to shop. The more variety of catalogs you have, the more fun the activity will be.

- *Vogue* magazine for excessive over-the-top clothes (note that *Vogue* also publishes *Teen Vogue)*
- Newport News—Newport News has a lot of immodest clothes, but they also have a large selection of stylish long skirts. www.newport-news.com
- Gap www.gap.com
- Abercrombie/ Fitch www.abercrombie.com

Find an article of clothing that:
- Is excessive/ over the top (contrary to Timothy passage)
- Would be appropriate at a fancy banquet
- Is ugly but in style
- Beautiful, but immodest for in public
- Is perfect but for one flaw (too low, too something) (must identify the flaw)
- Is too masculine (must identify why)
- Brings attention to one part of the body (must identify body part and why)

Questions for thought or discussion:
Name as many ways as you can think of why an outfit would be appropriate in one context but not the other.

_____
_____
_____

How do ladies in your age group most often reflect modesty/ immodesty? (give both)

_____

_____

_____

Name as many ways as you can think of that your love *for unsaved people* might change what you decide to wear.

_____

_____

_____

Name as many ways as you can think of that your love *for other believers* might change what you decide to wear.

_____

_____

_____

How can an outfit be modest but worn immodestly?

_____

_____

_____

How can you reflect God's character of humility and holiness in what you wear?

_____

_____

_____

_____

_____

For the teacher:

It can be helpful for teens who don't care about fashion to take a moment to look at what styles are up-to-date. Even if you do not want your teens looking like the world, teaching them to examine critically what the world is wearing can strengthen their own clothing choices.

For a teen who struggles with the desire to be fashion-conscious, critically examining the choices her peers are making and comparing them to God's standards can be especially helpful.

If you are doing an activity as a group, teach the girls how to make appropriate comments about other girls' answers. Examples: don't make negative comments about girls who might find thrift store shopping enjoyable, shop at Kmart or Wal-mart, or wear hand-me-downs.

Application 3

Practical Matters

Where do most teenagers go to shop for clothes (Christian or non-Christian)? Is this acceptable? Why or why not?

_____

_____

_____

What kinds of clothing are in style for teenagers right now? Is this type of dress acceptable? Are some items acceptable while others are not?

_____

_____

_____

What body part is being emphasized through clothes currently in style? (hint: what is tight, short, low, or see-through)

_____

_____

_____

What styles are hopelessly immodest? (e.g., short shorts)

_____

_____

_____

What styles can be combined with a classic piece of clothing to make a modest, up-to-date, outfit? (e.g., if long skirts are in style, match a long skirt with a blouse you already own)

_____

_____

_____

When do you think is the worst season to try to find modest clothes to buy (spring, summer, fall, winter)? Explain your answer.

_____

_____

_____

When do you think is the best time to try to find modest clothes to buy (spring, summer, fall, winter)? Explain your answer.

_____

_____

_____

What can you do if none of the current styles or colors look good on you?

_____

_____

_____

What do you think is the biggest struggle for Christian teenagers regarding modesty?

_____

_____

_____

_____

What could you say to a friend who struggles with being too concerned about what is in style or who struggles with being too concerned about having the prettiest clothing in her group of friends? In your answer, use Scripture that you have learned.

_____

_____

_____

_____

What could you say to a friend who struggles to follow the clothing rules of her family or school? In your answer, use Scripture that you have learned.

_____

_____

How do you respond when a friend asks for your opinion about an outfit that you think is ugly, doesn't look good on her, looks like grandma clothes, and so on?

_____

_____

_____

_____

Have you ever been told that something you wanted to wear or buy
was inappropriate? How did you respond? Was this a biblical response?

_____

_____

_____

_____

Modesty Verses

Humility

1 Peter 3:2-6—Whose adorning let it not be that outward adorning of plaiting the hair, and of wearing of gold, or of putting on of apparel; But let it be the hidden man of the heart, in that which is not corruptible, even the ornament of a meek and quiet spirit, which is in the sight of God of great price. For after this manner in the old time the holy women also, who trusted in God, adorned themselves, being in subjection unto their own husbands: Even as Sara obeyed Abraham, calling him lord: whose daughters ye are, as long as ye do well, and are not afraid with any amazement.

Micah 6:8—What does the Lord require of thee? But to do justly and to love mercy and to walk humbly [modestly] with thy God.

Proverbs 6:16-17—These six things doth the LORD hate: yea, seven are an abomination unto him: A proud look....

James 4:6-10—But he giveth more grace. Wherefore he saith, God resisteth the proud, but giveth grace unto the humble. Submit yourselves therefore to God. Resist the devil, and he will flee from you. Draw nigh to God, and he will draw nigh to you. Cleanse *your* hands, *ye* sinners; and purify *your* hearts, *ye* double minded. Be afflicted, and mourn, and weep: let your laughter be turned to mourning, and *your* joy to heaviness. Humble yourselves in the sight of the Lord, and he shall lift you up.

Acts 17:10-11—And the brethren immediately sent away Paul and Silas by night unto Berea: who coming thither went into the synagogue of the Jews. These were more noble than those in Thessalonica, in that they received the word with all readiness of mind, and searched the scriptures daily, whether those things were so.

Purity

Titus 2:4-5—That they may teach the young women to be sober, to love their husbands, to love their children, To be discreet, chaste, keepers at home, good, obedient to their own husbands, that the word of God be not blasphemed.

Purity should be reflected in all areas of our lives.
1 Peter 1:15—But as he which hath called you is holy, so be ye holy in all manner of conversation.

Hebrews 12:1—Wherefore seeing we also are compassed about with so great a cloud of witnesses, let us lay aside every weight, and the sin which doth so easily beset us, and let us run with patience the race that is set before us.

James 1:27— Pure religion and undefiled before God and the Father is this, To visit the fatherless and widows in their affliction, and to keep himself unspotted from the world.

Sexuality within the context of marriage is pure.
Proverbs 5:19—Let her [your wife] be as the loving hind and pleasant roe; let her breasts satisfy thee at all times ; and be thou ravished always with her love.

Hebrews 13:14—Marriage is honorable in all, and the bed undefiled.

Proverbs 31:11—The heart of her husband doth safely trust in her, so that he shall have no need of spoil.

The relationship between a husband and wife is a picture of the relationship between God and the believer.
Ephesians 5:31-32— For this cause shall a man leave his father and mother, and shall be joined unto his wife, and they two shall be one flesh. This is a great mystery: but I speak concerning Christ and the church.

Appropriateness

1 Timothy 2:9—In like manner also, that women adorn themselves in modest apparel, with shamefacedness and sobriety; not with braided hair, or gold, or pearls, or costly array; But (which becometh women professing godliness) with good works.

We must learn to evaluate each situation and decide how our clothing and actions are appropriate to the situation.

Proverbs 11:22—As a jewel of gold in a swine's snout, so is a fair woman which is without discretion.

Proverbs 16:20—He that handleth a matter wisely shall find good: and whoso trusteth in the LORD, happy *is* he.

Philippians 1:9-11—And this I pray, that your love may abound yet more and more in knowledge and in all judgment; That ye may approve things that are excellent; that ye may be sincere and without offence till the day of Christ; Being filled with the fruits of righteousness, which are by Jesus Christ, unto the glory and praise of God.

Romans 12:2—And be not conformed to this world: but be ye transformed by the renewing of your mind, that ye may prove what is that good, and acceptable, and perfect, will of God.

Ephesians 5:10—Proving what is acceptable unto the Lord.

1 Thessalonians 5:21—Prove all things; hold fast that which is good.

Hebrews 5:14—But strong meat belongeth to them that are of full age, even those who by reason of use have their senses exercised to discern both good and evil.

Fear of Man: Peer Pressure

Proverbs 29:25— The fear of man bringeth a snare: but whoso putteth his trust in the LORD shall be safe.

John 12:42-43—Nevertheless among the chief rulers also many believed on him; but because of the Pharisees they did not confess him, lest they should be put out of the synagogue: For they loved the praise of men more than the praise of God.

Our Testimony: Relationship to Others

Our actions are a testimony (good or bad) to unsaved and saved alike.

Matthew 5:14—Ye are the light of the world. A city that is set on a hill cannot be hid.

Romans 14:7,16,18-19—For none of us liveth to himself, and no man dieth to himself. Let not then your good be evil spoken of: For he that in these things serveth Christ is acceptable to God, and approved of men. Let us therefore follow after the things which make for peace, and things wherewith one may edify another.

Philippians 2:4—Look not every man on his own things, but every man also on the things of others.

We should be gracious toward those who disagree with us. If we believe we should confront a believer, we must first examine our own hearts.
Ephesians 4:3—Endeavor to keep the unity of the Spirit in the bond of peace.

Matthew 7:1-5—Judge not, that ye be not judged. For with what judgment ye judge, ye shall be judged: and with what measure ye mete, it shall be measured to you again. And why beholdest thou the mote that is in thy brother's eye, but considerest not the beam that is in thine own eye? Or how wilt thou say to thy brother, Let me pull out the mote out of thine eye; and, behold, a beam is in thine own eye? Thou hypocrite, first cast out the beam out of thine own eye; and then shalt thou see clearly to cast out the mote out of thy brother's eye.

1 Corinthians 13:4-7—Charity suffereth long, and is kind; charity envieth not; charity vaunteth not itself, is not puffed up, Doth not behave itself unseemly, seeketh not her own, is not easily provoked, thinketh no evil; Rejoiceth not in iniquity, but rejoiceth in the truth; Beareth all things, believeth all things, hopeth all things, endureth all things.

We should not break God's clear commands if asked to dress immodestly by an authority.

Acts 5:29—Then Peter and the other apostles answered and said, We ought to obey God rather than men.

We must ultimately leave others in God's hands, trusting that the Scripture we show them will accomplish God's will in His time and way.

Isaiah 55:11—So shall my word be that goeth forth out of my mouth: it shall not return unto me void, but it shall accomplish that which I please, and it shall prosper in the thing whereto I sent it.

Beauty

Proverbs 31:22—She maketh herself coverings of tapestry; her clothing is silk and purple.

Philippians 4:8—Finally, brethren, whatsoever things are true, whatsoever things are honest, whatsoever things are just, whatsoever things are pure, whatsoever things are lovely, whatsoever things are of good report; if there be any virtue, and if there be any praise, think on these things.

1 Corinthians 14:40—Let all things be done decently and in order.

God's temple, which represented His character, was beautiful. Our bodies are called God's temple. We should dress in such a way that reflects God's beauty and holiness.

Hebrews 8:5—Who serve unto the example and shadow of heavenly things, as Moses was admonished of God when he was about to make the tabernacle: for, See, saith he, *that* thou make all things according to the pattern shewed to thee in the mount.

1 Corinthians 6:19-20—What? know ye not that your body is the temple of the Holy Ghost which is in you, which ye have of God, and ye are not your own? For ye are bought with a price: therefore glorify God in your body, and in your spirit, which are God's.

Exodus 28:2—And thou shalt make holy garments for Aaron thy brother for glory and for beauty.

Psalm 29:2—Give unto the Lord the glory due unto his name; worship the Lord in the beauty of holiness.

Femininity

Femininity is the attitude of contentment with how God has made us as women.

Psalm 139:14—I will praise thee; for I am fearfully and wonderfully made: marvellous are thy works; and that my soul knoweth right well.

Psalm 34:8— O taste and see that the LORD is good: blessed is the man that trusteth in him.

Philippians 4:11— Not that I speak in respect of want: for I have learned, in whatsoever state I am, therewith to be content.

God desires the distinction between men and women to remain intact.

Deuteronomy 22:5—Differences in how we dress

1 Corinthians 11:14-15—Differences in our hair styles

Ephesians 5; Colossians 3:18-19—Differences in roles in the home

Genesis 1-2—Differences in how God created our bodies

Additional Resources

The following publications on modesty are all organized differently and have somewhat different emphases, and I believe they reflect a growing desire among evangelicals as well as conservative fundamentalists to dress according to biblical principles. It is refreshing to hear these women admit that dressing modestly is not "legalistic" but instead wise behavior for a Christian. Because different approaches will reach different people, a counselor may find these resources helpful. As well, the audio lessons by DeMoss may be valuable for a counselee who does not read well.

Those wishing to explore these resources further may find it helpful to understand how the approach in this book is somewhat different from them. Although I believe these differences are important, I still believe these resources can be valuable for some people. The biggest difference I see is the lack of emphasis on humility as a part of modesty. Although DeMoss and Hardy mention humility, it is not emphasized; and I believe humility is crucial in a modesty discussion. Another difference I see in this material is the mistaken idea that a woman dressing sensually with her husband is immodest, but godly. Immodesty is always sinful, so a definition of modesty must encompass appropriate times for dressing and acting sensually. Finally, although there is considerable overlap, readers may disagree on specific applications.

"Modesty: Does God Really Care What I Wear?"
Nancy Leigh DeMoss

http://www.reviveourhearts.com
This link is to a series of talks on modesty that many have found refreshing in tone and content. DeMoss discusses different aspects of modesty from a biblical perspective. DeMoss now sells a book titled *The Look* which addresses these issues as well. I have not read this book, so I cannot comment on it specifically.

"Modesty Matters"
Pam Hardy

http://www.biblebb.com/files/ModestyMatters.htm
This transcription of a lesson on modesty by Pam Hardy, one of the pastors' wives at Grace Community Church (where John MacArthur is the senior pastor) is well-balanced and gives specific problem

areas of dress. It also has a comprehensive checklist at the end that may be of use if it is not too overwhelming for a counselee.

Secret Keeper: The Delicate Power of Modesty
Dannah Gresh

This small book is written for teenagers and has an approach consistent with the one you find here. Gresh explains how our clothing choices affect men for better or worse. Because she comes from an evangelical perspective, some of her illustrations may be a problem for some readers. Gresh uses some CCM artists as positive role models for modest Christian dress. She also uses a nude statue as an example. The point she makes is good (and the illustrations are not gratuitous), but some readers may be uncomfortable with the illustration.

Gresh has some helpful modesty "tests" and a lesson plan for a fashion show on her website. Keep in mind that you may not agree with everything she says, but some of her ideas may be helpful for you.

http://www.purefreedom.org/blog/archives/000015.html (modesty tests)

http://www.purefreedom.org/blog/archives/000014.html (modesty fashion show)

Recovering Biblical Manhood & Womanhood: A Response to Evangelical Feminism
Edited by John Piper and Wayne A. Grudem (Crossway, 1991)

This comprehensive response to "Christian Feminism" explains the major portions of Scripture regarding gender roles, from head coverings to biblical submission. The discussions are scholarly, but not too technical for a diligent layperson. In general, this is a solid resource, although some chapters are better than others. To purchase or preview the book online, see http://www.cbmw.org/rbmw/

Bobbi Brown Teenage Beauty: Everything You Need to Look Pretty, Natural, Sexy and Awesome

Bobby Brown and Annemarie Iverson

The problem with many makeup books is that they do not distinguish between teenagers and older women. This book, written by a celebrity makeup artist, does a good job of emphasizing a natural look for teenagers. The before and after pictures do a good job of demonstrating small, subtle changes that make a positive difference in the appearance of teenagers. It does contain some references and pictures of "experimental makeup" and "prom beauty" along with occasional references to celebrities and their facial features or makeup styles. It is not associated with any fashion magazine (this is common among beauty/makeup books). This resource would be appropriate for a teenager with some discernment, or to read together with a trusted adult.

The Pocket Stylist: Behind-the-Scenes Expertise from a Fashion Pro on Creating Your Own Unique Look
Kendall Farr

This book helps women identify clothing that best fits their body shape. It does not have pictures (some illustrations). The emphasis of this book is more on developing your own style instead of being a slave to fashion trends that may not be flattering on your body. The author gives help choosing shirt-to-shoe styles and colors, underwear (gives her best choices of bras for each size, gives styles of panties that don't show lines), and accessories. She writes from a secular perspective and targets young women (not so much teenagers).

Inside Outside: A Fresh Look at Tzniut
Gila Manolson

This is a well-written book on modesty from an orthodox Jewish perspective directed to adults more than teenagers (her examples reflect this audience). While not the first book I would turn to on modesty, it has a positive tone and does contain helpful concepts, particularly when contrasting the inner person and the outer person. Because it is based more on common sense and intuitive modesty, beware of adopting Jewish standards as scriptural.

Modesty: An Adornment for Life
Rabbi Pesach Eliyahu Falk

This is an extensive and technical treatment of an orthodox Jewish perspective on modesty. (The book is printed in Israel and is full of Hebrew terminology.) I would recommend this book for anyone who is compelled to follow certain elements of modesty based on Jewish tradition. If you accept their view on some things (like sleeve length or head coverings), then you may be interested to know other elements as well (like avoiding the use of perfume in public or singing in front of men). Because a Jewish perspective on clothing is sometimes similar to a conservative Christian's, it is easy to forget that they do not have a good track record for properly interpreting the Scriptures.

$\mathcal{Q}$uestions to ask when purchasing clothing:

- Am I buying this clothing to please my friends?
- Am I spending too much time thinking about my clothing and how it relates to other people?
- Does it draw undue attention to sensual female areas?
- Can I alter the clothing in some way to correct any problems?
- Will it cause a godly young man to have difficulty keeping his thoughts pure?
- Is it distinctly feminine?
- Does this clothing fit the guidelines my authorities have set for me?
- Does it reflect a love for believers and un-believers I spend time with?
- Would a larger or smaller size look better?
- How does it look when I bend over, raise my arms, or sit down?

Take along card:

Cut along dotted line, place in purse or wallet to refer to when shopping for clothing.